COMMUNICATING WITH **CONFIDENCE**™

MAKING FRIENDS

THE ART OF SOCIAL NETWORKING IN LIFE AND ONLINE

JARED MEYER

ROSEN
PUBLISHING®

New York

To my best friends: you know who you are.

Published in 2012 by The Rosen Publishing Group, Inc.
29 East 21st Street, New York, NY 10010

Copyright © 2012 by The Rosen Publishing Group, Inc.

First Edition

Library of Congress Cataloging-in-Publication Data

Meyer, Jared.
Making friends: the art of social networking in life and online/Jared Meyer.
    p. cm.—(Communicating with confidence)
Includes bibliographical references and index.
ISBN 978-1-4488-5522-3 (library binding)—
ISBN 978-1-4488-5633-6 (pbk.)—
ISBN 978-1-4488-5634-3 (6-pack)
1. Friendship—Juvenile literature.
2. Online social networks—Juvenile literature.
I. Title.
BF575.F66M49 2012
158.2'5—dc22

                                                    2011013235

Manufactured in the United States of America

CPSIA Compliance Information: Batch #W12YA: For further information, contact Rosen Publishing, New York, New York, at 1-800-237-9932.

CONTENTS

INTRODUCTION

Making friends has never been more important, more popular, more exciting, and more overwhelming. People now have constant access to millions of people worldwide through technologies such as social media. People from within our communities, throughout our cities, or even around the world are open to connecting with others online. And while such a fun, never-ending opportunity may inspire people to make more and more friends, at what point will they realize that the friends they meet online probably won't satisfy them the same way offline friends can? At what point in their search for new friends will they recognize that their unyielding quest to meet new people won't end until they're satisfied with the friends they make beyond the Internet?

There are several important differences between friendships in life and online. Online friendships may not be as strong or satisfying because they offer only a fraction of what friendships in life can offer. These friendships are generally limited to a few different ways of communicating. They're also usually just limited to sharing content. Friendships

Friendships in real life provide people of all ages rich and unique experiences that aren't available online. Communicating via the Internet, however, can make these relationships even more fun.

in life, however, include not only those fun and interesting experiences but so much more. In life, the friendships you have with others are often based on truly sharing your lives together.

The more friends you make, the more you'll learn about friendship firsthand. You will learn that there are different types of friends. You will also find that there can be some significant differences between meeting people in life and meeting them online. People won't know what will happen when they meet new people until they try. Meeting new people offers no guarantees, but most people will probably tell you that making the effort is usually worth the risk. There are so many great benefits of making new friends and rarely anything to lose by trying.

The purpose of this book is to highlight some good tips for forming profound, long-lasting, highly satisfying, and healthy relationships—these are the types of friendships that can help people grow academically, personally, professionally, and socially. Making friends is more of an art than a science. There is no one perfect approach to meeting new people. Each person may have his or her own personal approach to making friends. Whether you're meeting someone new in person or online, there will always be an opportunity to develop better relationships.

FRIENDSHIP BASICS

While the topic of friendship is something that is not taught in school, most people know the importance and at least a few benefits of friendship. At the very least, most people usually know that friendships offer them companionship and fun experiences. Some other benefits often include sharing personal and professional contacts as well as business or career opportunities.

You may be familiar with the expression "You can never have too many friends." Given the amount of time we have in our daily lives, however, some of our friendships may be more like acquaintances. Have you ever heard about the trade-off between quality and quantity? That "less is more"? It's easy to notice that the more connections you have, the less you're able to give everyone an equal share of your time, effort, and focus. And the less available you are, the more likely that some of the relationships you maintain won't be as strong as others.

The overall experience of making friends will be easier to manage and enjoy when you completely understand a few fundamental aspects of friendship. This chapter provides you with the important information you need in order to both prepare for and protect yourself when connecting with new people.

The Different Types of Friends

Not only is making friends more of an art than a science, but maintaining a friendship itself is an art, too. That's because there is no one official way to approach this type of relationship. When it comes to evaluating the different types of friendships that you may have in your lifetime, there is a wide spectrum that may exist. On one end of the spectrum may be the people

whom you met just once and haven't connected with since. On the other end of the spectrum may be the people with whom you have shared consistent, strong, lifelong friendships. These may be the friendships you've had for many years, perhaps since you were a child.

Many people never forget their first friendships. Thanks to social networking sites, they have the ability to stay connected with friends from their childhood.

Scattered throughout the spectrum, you may find childhood friends whom you have known since you were younger. You may or may not currently be in contact with them. If you do keep in touch, you may not currently be considered very close. Close friends may be thought of as those with whom you consistently keep in touch. These may be the friends whom you care about more than others.

Your best friends may be those people with whom you are currently the closest and share your life experiences with the most. Alternatively, your acquaintances may be people whom you have met only once or twice and with whom you have an inconsistent relationship. These are the types of people that would be pretty easy to reach if for any reason you wanted to connect with them. And finally, connections may be those people whom you've met once and have rarely, barely, or never even connected with since the first time you both met.

As you can see, there are so many ways to categorize friends. The examples above are just one way to figure out the differences between friends. They emphasize that one type of friendship can sometimes be much different from the other. Each friendship can have unique components such as when you met, how you met, how long you've been friends, how close you are, how often you communicate, and how you share experiences together. Therefore, the term "best friend" may mean something different to you than it does to another person. The shared experiences and length of time you've known another person often form the foundation for the type of relationship that you have with someone.

Benefits of Building Relationships

Forging new relationships can help you in many ways, both personally and professionally. Here are a few benefits of making new friends:

- **Personal growth:** People sometimes learn to become better human beings just by interacting with friends. Friendships allow two people to challenge and support each other and to sometimes even help each do things better.

- **Sharing:** Sharing is a big part of friendship. Sharing similar and sometimes different interests can be highly enjoyable.

- **Social support:** Sometimes people prefer to be with friends rather than their own family during difficult times.

- **Communication:** People can improve their communication skills just by sharing informal conversations with their friends.

- **Opportunities:** Having relationships with people automatically makes you a priority to them. This often will give you instant access to valuable opportunities. Friends are usually one of the first types of people invited to join others on trips or to see live entertainment.

Where to Meet People

Given the popularity of the Internet and social networking Web sites such as Facebook, which has hundreds of millions of members, practically anyone with an Internet connection and basic computer skills can make friends online. People can make

Meeting people sometimes happens randomly without any planning at all. You can make friends just by asking to participate in an activity or by inviting others to join you.

friends anytime of the day or night from practically anywhere in the world. And while making friends online may often appear to be more convenient compared to making friends in life, there's nothing quite like meeting new people in person. Meeting people in the flesh offers a more personal and complete experience. Such an experience leads people to enjoy higher levels of satis-faction both personally and socially.

There are several differences between meeting friends online and making friends face-to-face. Making friends in real life allows you to quickly judge a person's character by his or her behavior. It also helps you evaluate how a person treats you and others. It even allows you to see for yourself if he or she is able to communicate naturally in person. This is because you're sharing a part of your lives together and not just an electronic communication. Online communication can sometimes be edited and crafted to sound just right. Talking in person, however, is more personal and natural.

Compared to meeting in person, there are usually limitations to connecting with someone online. For example, there's only so much you can share online. Often, only text, images, and videos can be shared between two people over the Internet. Using video conferencing services can help make connecting with someone online for the first time more personal and human, but taking the time to do that is rare. There's just nothing quite like making friends in person.

Staying Safe

Would you be more likely to trust someone you met in person or someone you met online? Sometimes meeting people online provides less certainty about their real personality, true identity, and real intentions. Upon meeting people online, you may never be able to verify their true identity, especially when they don't live in the same area as you. Just as you'd never share private information with someone you met in person, the same can be said about meeting people online. You may never know if the new friends that you make on social networking sites such as Facebook are truly who they say they are. Of course, this may eventually be proved by sharing more interactions and communications. Still, you may never really know what a person is truly like if you don't meet him or her in person.

Understanding Your Needs

Throughout the course of people's lives, they will always have different reasons for wanting to make new friends. Some people may want to make new friends in order to find a new job or entrepreneurial opportunity. Others may want to meet new people because they recently became interested in a new activity like hiking. They may have realized that the experience would be so much better with a hiking partner. Yet another reason why others may want a new friend is to connect on a deeper level with someone and give and receive support.

Social networking sites make it easy to meet with old friends who wish to experience real-life activities together, such as hiking.

There are numerous reasons why anyone would like to make new friends. Some people have only one objective, whereas others may want more in a friendship than simply sharing activities together.

People sometimes value their friendships differently and may have different expectations with regard to their friendships. The sooner they understand and accept this and the fact that they may not always be able to offer what a new friend wants or needs (and vice versa), the easier it will be to make new friends. Sometimes you just can't force a new friendship. For example, imagine meeting someone with whom you have great chemistry. While everything may seem perfect, you may then come to realize that you really don't have time to contribute to such an amazing person. Or you may decide that spending less time with another friend in order to get to know this new person may not be worth it at the present time. One of the great things about friendship is that there is rarely an urgency to commit to starting a new one. Sometimes it may make sense to keep in touch with someone great that you've met and perhaps build upon your new friendship at a later time.

Working Through Your Differences

The more you can relate to someone that you've recently met, the more likely it is that you'll desire to be friends with him or her. However, people with very different personalities can still have remarkable friendships. What people need to understand when

People are sometimes pleasantly surprised and delighted to realize that some of their strongest friendships are with people very different from themselves.

it comes to making friends with others that have vastly different personalities is that no two people will ever be exactly alike. People are unique and they will often see, want, and do things differently. People rarely share the same perspective, and when it comes to their preferences, well, they all usually know what they like. This means they will often commit to what they like, even if it's very different from what others prefer. Additionally, people have different priorities. Their personal lives, schedules, and obligations to other people will be pretty dynamic. And yet, most people are still not only able to get along but also share some great friendships with people very different from themselves.

Setting expectations about making friends that are realistic will make getting along with different people easier. If everyone were exactly like you, you'd probably get bored pretty quickly. Despite people's basic personality differences, two friends with very different and even conflicting beliefs, values, and goals can still get along well and have a great time together. What's their secret? The more fundamental values related to friendship that they share, the more likely they will be able to build a great friendship.

SOCIAL NETWORKING: ONLINE AND OFFLINE

There will always be opportunities to meet new people and make friends. If you live in a small town, you can make friends in person and online. If you live in a big city, you can make friends in any of the variety of venues the city affords. And even if you don't have an Internet connection, you can still make friends everywhere you go. Yet, even while knowing that there is always going to be an opportunity to connect with someone somewhere, making friends doesn't have to be an overwhelming experience. Sure, if you treat making friends seriously, you could potentially connect with new people each day.

One of the most exciting times in the life of a friendship often occurs during the beginning stages of the relationship.

However, taking such an intensive approach to meeting new people can be overwhelming. This is especially true when you try to attempt to manage more relationships than you can handle. That's especially hard to do while tending to other priorities and obligations in your life. In the first chapter, you learned that understanding the fundamentals of friendship prepares people to get along with new friends. This chapter will cover a few important aspects of meeting new people for the very first time as well as during your first few interactions.

One of the things that can make meeting new people less daunting is the fact that there are two factors over which we have little or any control: chemistry and compatibility. In order to consider building a new friendship, it will be critically important to have both chemistry and compatibility with someone you've just met. These are two powerful components to relationships that can rarely be faked or forced. Without these two basic but important ingredients, the likelihood of a friendship forming is pretty low.

Chemistry

Personal chemistry between two people can be described as being on the same wavelength as each other. This is when they have easy and free-flowing conversations. This is also apparent when they share a similar sense of humor. Two people with a strong amount of personal chemistry usually often just "get" each other. No one can produce personal chemistry between two people in a science lab. It is the one ingredient that will either make or break a new connection. Additionally, there is no specific formula for how much chemistry two people need in order to motivate them to develop a friendship. Upon meeting, two people will usually be able to tell if they're interested in building something deeper with one another based on their initial interactions.

Some people believe that chemistry can't develop over time like its counterpart, compatibility. They may say, "Either you've got it or you don't" and prefer not to keep in touch with another person if the connection isn't strong enough from the very start. Other people may believe that chemistry between two people can evolve over time. They may believe that they may get along better at some point in the future. And so, they may become better acquainted another time. Either way, it always comes down to a personal choice: do you choose to invest in new relationships with people with whom you have remarkable chemistry, or do you try to make things work with practically anyone with whom you think you could be friends?

Compatibility

Compatibility is based on how many things you have in common with someone else, whether they are perceptions, preferences, or even priorities. Often, the more you have in common with someone, the more likely you are to relate to him or her. However, you can still be compatible with someone who sees, wants, likes, and does things very differently than you. Unlike chemistry, compatibility is more likely to evolve over time. In fact, it may take just one or two changes in people's lives to allow them to relate more or better to someone that they know. While our fundamental personalities rarely change over the course of our lives, we usually have the ability to make both minor and major modifications here and there to our behavior. Any number of changes to one's perceptions, preferences, and priorities can bring two people closer. If a friend's personality changes dramatically, however, it can also pull the two people apart.

Imagine for a moment that you meet a number of new people in person or online over the course of thirty days. What are the chances that you'll have a high level of chemistry and compatibility with any of them? Even if you were to meet one hundred new people a day in person within one month, it's likely that you would have things in common with at least a few of them. The probability that you'll have great chemistry

Having extremely strong chemistry and compatibility with a new friend can make it seem as though you've known each other forever.

with them is pretty unlikely, however. While the supply of people that you can become friends with is abundant, strong chemistry between two people is typically very rare because it's the unique result of two personalities making a great match.

To make a great first impression, a few extremely attractive traits people can have are a healthy level of confidence, the capability of being cooperative, and, not surprisingly, great communication skills. These three things encourage people to share a decent initial interaction and possibly move toward developing a new friendship. You may have heard the expression, "You never get a second chance to make a good first impression." As obvious as it sounds, this phrase emphasizes the fact that people may make firm judgments about you based on your behavior and appearance during your very first interaction with them.

Confidence

Having a healthy level of confidence is very attractive to people because it shows that you're self-secure. This also allows them to assume that you're content with who you are and where you are in your life. Furthermore, confidence also often conveys that you have a strong, resilient personality. Confident people are more often protected from uncomfortable things like personal criticism or

Unnecessary arguments can be avoided completely between two friends when both cooperate and communicate openly and respectfully with each other.

even fear and doubt. A healthy level of confidence will always be considered attractive when you appear assertive and even courageous. Whereas bragging is usually considered a turnoff to most people, you can be modest (and sometimes even self-deprecating) in conversation and still appear confident.

Cooperation

It's easy to be friends with people you easily get along with. You may meet some fantastic people whom you'd love to get to know better. What may quickly change your mind, however, is when you start to recognize the signs that it would probably be difficult (and even sometimes near impossible) to be friends with them. This may be due to their unique personality and uncooperative nature. People like others who aren't demanding and are simply easy to be around.

Communication

Communication is considered by many people to be the foundation of building and maintaining rela-tionships. Without healthy communication, you've got nothing more than someone in the same room as you. Having such a companion is like not having a companion at all. The better your com-panion is at communicating, the easier it will be to develop a friendship with him or her. This includes both written and verbal communication. Whether you approach someone at a party to start a conversation or send someone an initial e-mail, what you say and how you say it will matter immensely.

We've learned that being confident and cooperative while being able to communicate effectively is important when meeting new people and trying to establish new friendships. Assuming you've got a good level of chemistry with someone you've just met and that you have a few things in common, there are three more traits that most people find very appealing in new friends.

Approachability

If you were to meet someone who avoids eye contact and doesn't smile, it would be highly unlikely that you (or anyone) would be interested in starting a conversation with him or her. Approachability is another word for being friendly. When you appear open to talking to other people, you allow others to approach you, whether it's to start a conversation about the

Friendships are meant to be fun. It's very easy to start a conversation with most people when you're approachable.

book you're holding or even to ask you for the time. Such a light approach to starting a conversation allows two people to make an initial connection and establish rapport. This allows them to feel each other out and decide whether they want to get to know each other better. Sometimes all you need is one thing in common to start a conversation. At the very least, all it may take to start a conversation is a smile. It's one of the things many people have in common when they're interested in making friends.

Authenticity

How compatible two people are is usually based on how much they can identify and relate to each other. This is normally and naturally done by considering one's own identity and comparing it to another's. When two people who have just met act naturally and behave as normally as they would in any other social environment, they can tell that their conversation and intentions are authentic. Being authentic means being genuine. This is easy to do when you're secure with who you are and relatively comfortable being vulnerable when connecting with someone new.

Inquisitiveness

One of the most attractive things anyone can do when meeting someone new is having a healthy dose of curiosity, or inquisitiveness. Without being curious about people you've just met, it's often difficult to get to know them unless they're naturally an open and assertive communicator. If they're not particularly open (or even curious) themselves, the conversation could quickly come to an end. This may prove that one or both of you has difficulty meeting new people or that one of you is simply not interested in talking further.

One of the easiest ways to show people that you're genuinely interested in getting to know them is by asking questions. Authentic, appropriate questions that allow you to share an enjoyable conversation may lead to future conversation. Asking questions also allows you to learn about their background, interests, goals, and even values. The more open you are to being asked questions, the easier it will be to get to know you, too. Starting a conversation with someone can be super easy.

MYTHS and facts

MYTH
The best relationships are easy.

fact

In a perfect world, everyone would always get along, treat each other extremely well, and consistently enjoy each other's company. Therefore, managing relationships would be super easy. In reality, though, there is no simple approach to having great, long-lasting relationships.

MYTH
You can never have too many friends.

fact

You can never have too many connections, but given that friendships require (and offer) so much more than casual connections do, it is pretty impossible to have close, consistent, and healthy relationships with an unlimited number of people. A person's available time can often be limited. Even having a few hundred online friends is nothing like having two or three amazing friendships in real life.

MYTH
The older you get, the harder it is to make new friends.

fact

The more experience people have attempting to build new relationships, the easier it will be to meet new people in the future. Making friends is often considered a life-long skill because friendships can come and go, sometimes without any warning whatsoever. While many people may still have strong, lifelong friendships later on in their lives, there will always be new opportunities to make new friends. For example, moving to a new place or developing new interests are just two great reasons why anyone at any age may wish to make new friends.

DEVELOPING NEW CONTACTS

S o far you've learned about both the fundamentals of friendship and the basics to meeting new people. This chapter will review a few additional skills that you can use to develop much stronger relationships with your new friends.

A friendship can become as strong as both friends want it to become. The relationship can become stronger slowly over time or grow over a relatively short period. As previously mentioned, there is rarely an urgency to ever build a friendship with someone. Sometimes you just don't know what's in store for the friendship either. In

Trust is an essential part of any strong relationship and is built by working together cooperatively.

fact, you may meet people in life or online and communicate with them inconsistently during the next month or so. However, a few months or even years down the line, you may eventually become great friends.

Skills for stronger friend-ships, such as teamwork, keeping commitments, and generosity, may be experienced during the beginning stages of meeting someone new. They are usually expected and even more important, however, as the friendship develops over time. In fact, these are just a few things that not only bring two people closer but also prove to one another that their relationship is important. Sometimes it can also show that their friendship is one of the most important ones that they've got.

Teamwork and Trust

While "teamwork" may be a word that you rarely see or hear being used when referring to friendship, a friendship can be considered very much like a team. The two team members have a shared goal as well as a personal stake in the prog-ress, experiences, and outcomes of their relatively small group. When you approach friendships like they are teams, it helps remind you to behave as if the friendship is never just about you. It also reaffirms that you're not the only one who benefits from the relationship. Furthermore, it reminds you that you're also not the only one who has something to lose. Like any team of which you're a member, the more time and effort that you contribute to the group, the more valuable it will become. This is why the longer you have a friendship with someone, the more special it will be and the more you will trust each other.

Trustworthiness is determined by how reliable and honest you think someone is in a friendship. When it comes to trust, the longer you and your friends have had a relationship, the deeper the level of trust you share will be. And so, it's very rare that people will trust each other very much upon meeting for the first time. In fact, it's very common that they may not trust each other at all. This is perfectly normal because trust is usually earned and experienced over time. One of the fastest ways to develop trust is to try and find out about a person's past. There are no guarantees that someone's previous actions will predict his or her future behaviors. However, it's better to know if someone has a history

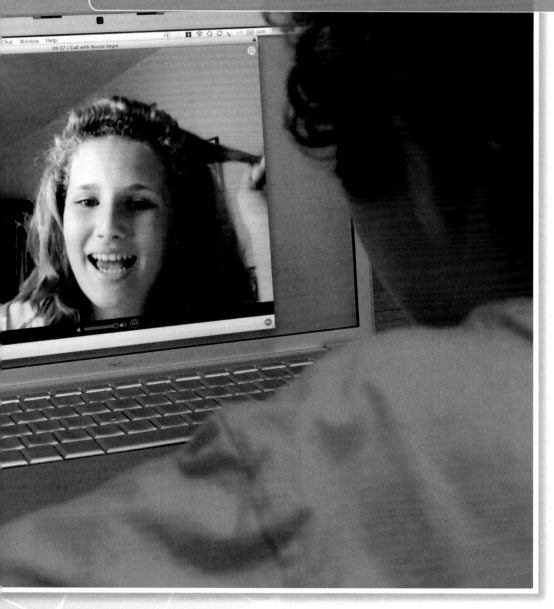

Sharing video conferences with friends is usually a lot more intimate than sharing phone calls or an instant messaging session. Live video requires each user's complete attention.

of being honest or untrustworthy. It would be good to find out sooner rather than later if your new friends may not necessarily be trustworthy with regard to specific things like keeping secrets or borrowing money.

Developing trust with a new friend can begin quickly when someone you know referred your new friend to you. Furthermore, anytime through-out the friendship, you could always ask the friend you have in common about your new friend's trustworthi-ness. This could be about anything from sharing private information to sharing personal property.

Keeping Commitments

One component of developing trust in a relationship is one's willingness and ability to keep commitments. This could mean agreeing to meet your new friend at a specific place and time or agreeing to do or not do something. Keeping commitments is one of the most important aspects of a friendship. Priorities and obligations are known for changing throughout our hectic lives, and sometimes we have to change or even cancel our commitments.

Your actions speak for themselves. Keeping commitments is essential when you truly care about those you call your friends.

However, if a consistent pattern forms where a person in the friendship has difficulty keeping commitments, the quality of the relationship will most likely suffer. If too many commitments are broken over a relatively short period of time, it may be difficult

Managing Your Generosity

Given that sharing is a big part of friendship, it's one reason why having no more than a few strong friendships may be all anyone needs, wants, or can even manage to maintain. None of us can be everything to everyone because there's only so much we're capable of giving to people. There's also only so much we can do within a normal day. It's easy to remember that the more friends you have, the more you have to put into the friendships. This always includes generosity and sharing. Just like having a relatively well-balanced life is healthy, so is having a manageable number of friendships. How many friends a person has is a personal choice. Since we can't share everything with everybody, having just a few friends will probably be both easier and more satisfying to you. Even one or two strong friendships may be all you need at this time in your life.

What happens when one person is more generous in a friendship than the other? It will depend on the quality of the relationship and the preferences and expectations of each person. Some friendships may be more focused on one person than the other. Other friendships may be perfectly balanced where each contributes an equal amount of things to the relationship. Because generosity and sharing take so many different forms, it may be impossible to determine if two friends share equally and fairly. For example, it's pretty hard to compare the value of four small favors in one week to one big gift during the same month. When something like sharing doesn't seem or feel right, bring it up during your next conversation with your friend. You'll probably figure out the concern pretty quickly and know what changes your friendship may need.

to regain the trust that has been lost. Unfortunately, friendships aren't invincible and there's only so much disappointment that one can take before deciding that it's no longer worth trying to be friends with someone. In the end, one's failure to keep commitments may be the very thing that ends a friendship if the disappointed friend isn't very committed to the friendship. Alternatively, even the strongest commitment to a friendship won't necessarily change because of a friend's consistently disappointing behavior.

How do you determine how sensitive your friends are about keeping commitments with them? The easiest way to figure this out is to ask them casually about their preferences. It's really the only way to find out what their expectations are from the friendship. Keep in mind that each friendship is different, and even if you've heard from a mutual friend that your new friend always keeps his or her commitments, that may only be so in the other friendship.

Discussing personal preferences in a friendship is also one of the ways you can lay the groundwork for the rest of your relationship. The sooner two people communicate their preferences with regard to the type of friendship they want, the sooner disappointment can be prevented. While you may think you can tell how flexible someone may by thinking about their general nature (laid-back, rigid, etc.), it's always smarter to ask rather than assume.

For example, when it comes to getting together, you may have friends that are pretty particular about meeting at a specific time. To them, "2:00 PM" may literally mean "2:00 PM on the dot." Alternatively, "2:00 PM" to one friend may mean "Around 2:00 PM" or even, "Sometime between 2:00 PM and 2:15 PM." It's even likely that you have a friend who prefers that "2:00 PM" mean "Sometime after 2:00 PM."

When it comes to making commitments like meeting up in person or online, people can always at least try to accommodate their friends' lifestyles and personalities. This is where compromising comes into play. Let's say that you're usually laid-back and your friend is rigid: you can both still work out a way to make plans to get together without causing anyone disappointment. Once you're able to set reasonable expectations, you can usually make appropriate arrangements and maintain a relatively harmonious friendship.

Sharing

Generosity and sharing make friendships fun and interesting. People usually have very unique styles of giving. They also probably have particular preferences about receiving certain things

Sharing interesting and entertaining content, such as photos, with friends via social networking sites is a good way to mix online and offline socializing.

as well. There are usually only three ways people can find out what their friends like when it comes to giving and receiving: (1) by guessing (which can be risky), (2) by asking someone they know, or (3) the direct way, by simply asking what their

43

friends prefer. Two additional factors that usually come into play include the quality of the friendship and timing. Generosity can be experienced by lending one's personal property, giving gifts (whether virtual or physical), helping someone out, spending time together, or even giving a compliment.

You may prefer spending time with a friend rather than doing favors for him or her. In turn, your friend may prefer giving you sincere compliments rather than giving you gifts. Either way, it's important to recognize and understand one's ability for and interest in generosity. It also helps to know why people give what they do and, when appropriate, what they prefer to receive. Sharing images or videos online with friends in life or online will probably be easier and more convenient than doing something together with them. Even sharing something in person may take more work than doing so online. However, no matter how many photos, videos, or funny jokes you e-mail a friend, sometimes it just doesn't compare to spending time together. To some people, spending just thirty minutes together working on a shared project or helping each other do errands is more satisfying than communicating and sharing online.

The expression "It's the thought that counts" makes sense when you have some idea of what your friends would prefer receiving from you. For example, ordering a book on a topic that you like and sending it to your friends may be considered generous, but not necessarily thoughtful. That is, of course, if it's a book you'd like to share with them because it's something that you think they may enjoy or benefit from. If knowing what your friends would most likely appreciate doesn't come quickly to you, give it some thought.

Make sure you think of your friends when you're interested in sharing something with them. Asking yourself, "What do I know he or she would love?" will always be more effective than asking yourself, "What do I think he or she could like?" When in doubt, ask—even if it may ruin the surprise. Besides, you can always ask way in advance of giving someone something. You can also ask someone else they know what type of things your friends would enjoy receiving.

CHAPTER 4

MAINTAINING YOUR FRIENDSHIPS

Amazing friendships rarely blossom overnight. They take time to develop, whether it is over the course of a month, a year, or even several years. The best of friendships develop naturally, and at some random point, it usually becomes clear that the two people wish to consider themselves as best friends. Sometimes, however, only one of the two friends may consider the other his or her best friend, since the feelings may not be exactly the same.

Some people may think that you can only truly have one best friend. Others believe that you can have more than one best friend. Either way, if the relationship is fantastic and the two of you are really close, there's really no need to stress yourself out over categorizing your friends. Sometimes you just know what you've got with someone and categorizing it won't really make a difference. When this happens, you know you've got a pretty amazing friendship. What is it that causes the best of friends to have such amazing relationships? One's

Close friends are some of the most important people in our lives. Some people may have one very close friend while others may have more.

best friends are usually considered the most important friends in his or her life. That says a lot about a person's character. This chapter will cover a few important skills that often lead two people to potentially become amazing friends.

When friends don't communicate with compassion and respect, conflict can arise. Being honest and direct without being hurtful can help prevent relationship problems.

The more you care about someone, the more likely you'll consciously try to invest in your friendship and prevent conflict. This section covers a few important ways to express how much you value your friends when you interact with them in person or on the Internet. By following these methods, the friendship will naturally thrive as well.

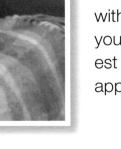

Being Honest and Direct

The longer you know people, the easier it usually is to be honest and direct with them. This is because being honest and direct with people can sometimes be difficult. Not everyone will agree with your opinions. And when people hear your opinions and don't necessarily agree with them, they may quickly become defensive or even angry in order to protect themselves from criticism. Is it ever really OK to be dishonest with a friend? How about a close one? There are tactful ways to be honest with someone without criticizing or complaining. It's also not just what you say that matters, but also how you say it. If you're good friends with people, it would only make sense that you should be comfortable sharing your honest thoughts with them. Hopefully, you'd also appreciate receiving the truth in return.

Acting Appropriately and Respectfully

While it's safe to assume that friends will treat each other well, sometimes one of you may accidentally or even intentionally do or say something hurtful. When it comes to a friendship, who's to judge if what you do or say is right or wrong? If you know your friends well, you'll probably be able to tell what type of comments or actions will probably be considered offensive or hurtful to them. It's sometimes easy to lose control when you're playing around or even poking some fun at good friends. While you never have to feel like you're "walking on eggshells" when you're interacting with friends, it's really important to remember always to try to make positive contributions to a friendship.

A quick way to size up a friendship is to evaluate how much appreciation, consideration, and effort you both contribute to the relationship. The more you and your friend appreciate each other, are considerate of each other's needs and wants, and make an effort to maintain a friendship, the better chance your relationship will last well into the future.

Being Appreciative

Saying "thank you" is a pretty standard practice that usually comes naturally to people. Beyond having the good manners that most people would expect of you, being appreciative of your friends can be really easy to express. How often do you hear friends say how much they appreciate having you in their lives? How often do you hear them tell you what they admire about you? It may be difficult for some people to share such gratitude with others.

Being taken for granted is one of the fastest ways to dissolve a friendship, whereas sharing one's appreciation will usually bring two good friends even closer together.

Being appreciative may make them feel vulnerable. Therefore, they may feel that not saying anything prevents possibly getting rejected. Alternatively, sharing one's appreciation may also bring friends closer, and this may be something a friend may not be comfortable doing. The fact remains, however, that people (especially those in friendships) crave appreciation and approval. Being told you're important by your online acquaintances can feel great, but hearing you're important to your closest friends in life can feel amazing. Gratitude helps friendships flourish, especially when it's shared.

Being Considerate

Saying "please" is another standard way of being kind to others, but a lot more is expected between great friends. Being considerate is easy to do when you remember that your friendship is a team where each member considers the other's needs and wants as much as their own. Sure, sending a thank-you note can be considered thoughtful and considerate after a friend does something special for you. Yet there are so many more creative ways to be considerate in return. Being considerate usually proves to people that you're not taking them for granted, since you're doing or saying something that shows that you value them.

Making an Effort

The health of a friendship can change at any time. Sometimes it may be exciting, sometimes it may just exist, and at other times

Compassion and Care

It's easy to assume that people must care about others in order to call them friends. Some people, however, can sometimes consider people friends yet would not care if they completely disappeared from their lives the next day. It's normal to care differently about different friends. There are some friends you may care about deeply, while there are other friends you may not care about much at all. Friendship is based on love, and the love you have for a friend is the result of how much compassion and care you feel toward them.

"Compassion" is another word for "sympathy" or simply concern with regard to another person's situation or circumstances. Imagine a friend of yours is suffering from a minor illness like a cold, or something much worse like a close family member dying. How you react to the news can quickly tell you how you feel about and relate to the issue. Additionally, what you say, and especially how you empathize with your friend, can say a lot about you. It will reflect your personality, how you relate to your friend, and how much he or she means to you.

Some people are more emotional than others. Others may be considered less caring. There are also people who may come across as too caring. Do you consider yourself a deeply emotional person? There's no perfect way to feel or behave when you learn that a friend is dealing with a difficult issue or life event. Furthermore, you don't need to struggle with how you feel about hearing bad news. Some people are resilient to most unfortunate circumstances, whereas others may need emotional support during rough times. What's most important is that you be a supportive friend.

it may be exhausted. A friendship may even be on the verge of ending. What you and your friends contribute to your friendship today will determine where it ends up tomorrow. Making an effort in a friendship can be compared to the human heart. Friendships blossom each time effort is made between friends. The higher the quality of contributions that each of you contributes, the healthier and stronger a friendship will be. However, it's natural for a bond between two friends to fluctuate over time. Again, because making friends is more of an art than it is a science, there is no perfect formula for maintaining a perfect relationship.

Being Understanding

One of the most effective ways to manage relationships with people is to know how to respond and react to them. This includes the times when they do things like you would or differently than you would. Knowing when and how to understand, accept, and forgive friends often helps prevent conflict, deepen intimacy, and build an even stronger friendship.

Being understanding won't necessarily mean that you will always know why a friend does or says something differently than you would normally do or say. It simply means being able to fully recognize that you and your friend are unique individuals. Also, it means that while you may have some or even many things in common, you both will still have many significant differences. When it comes to making plans with friends, for example, one friend may prefer to use the phone whereas another may prefer to text or even use e-mail. When you completely understand that your friends have perceptions, preferences, and priorities that are often different from yours, it's so much easier to get along with them.

Friendships can be maintained both in person and through social networking tools, such as standard computers and smartphones.

Being Accepting

There are a lot of things in people's lives and friendships that they can't control. When things occur that they would rather not have experienced, it can be frustrating to deal with the consequences. Learning to allow your friends to be themselves can help keep the friendship real. It also takes the pressure off of you to resist or even change your friends. Your friends are going to make mistakes, say the wrong things, do silly things, or even do things that you could do or have done so much better. While many people may enjoy the power of personal development, it's often better to accept your friends for who they are rather than try to change them and make them become someone else. Besides, it's easier to help someone change when they truly want to make personal changes in their life.

Being Forgiving

When things don't go as planned or exactly as you may like it, it probably makes sense just to say, "I understand, accept, and forgive my friends for their choices and behavior." However, when it comes to forgiveness, it's not always that easy. Being forgiving means completely releasing any concerns, criticism, disappointment, and even anger related to a specific action, event, or experience for which someone is directly responsible. In order to forgive friends for something they did that upset you, telling yourself you forgive them will probably not make much of a difference. Even if you believe it to be true, it probably won't be enough.

True forgiveness takes place by completely releasing resentful thoughts when you talk about the issue with your friends. You don't have to request that they change. You don't even need to request an apology. It's highly suggested, however, that to truly forgive your friends, you tell them in person that you forgive them and why. Otherwise, you may hold hidden resentment and anger toward them. Completely forgiving someone can seem difficult, but you can laugh about it even while doing it. Forgiveness can be one of the hardest parts of friendship.

10 Great Questions
TO ASK A PSYCHOLOGIST

1. Why are important subjects like making friends and building relationships not formally taught in schools?

2. What are some icebreakers that I can use to get to know others?

3. How can I go about starting a friendship club at school for those interested in meeting students that are new?

4. What do you think are a few good reasons to start making new friends?

5. What are a few easy ways for a new student to make friends at school?

6. What do you think is the secret to lifelong friendships?

7. Do adults usually have an easier or harder time making new friends?

8. Why do some new friends randomly disappear from our lives?

9. Do you suggest not pursuing a new friendship with someone who's known for being difficult?

10. How can people build confidence and protect themselves from experiencing rejection?

BUILDING LIFELONG RELATIONSHIPS

People have the freedom to make new friends throughout their lives. Whether it's during school or college, at work, during retirement, or even later in life, new friends can be made. While some lifelong friendships may never be consistent, there is always the possibility of rekindling a friendship in the future. Given that people are more accessible in the twenty-first century, making friends can sometimes be considered highly competitive. Since there will always be new friends to make, the ones you've known the longest will sometimes be even more important to you.

Lifelong friendships are often considered the most valuable because of how long two people have known each other. Sometimes, the longer the friendship, the stronger the bond.

Compared to the twentieth century, there are more opportunities to make new friends. Also, there are plenty of opportunities to replace even our newest friends as well. This chapter will discuss the very special nature of life-long friendships. It can be fulfilling just knowing someone for many years. It can also be even more special when you've shared a consistent friendship throughout that time. Being loyal and treating your most valued friends like they're family members are two ways to ensure that the friendship flourishes. The more you naturally want to treat friends like they're family members, the more likely you'll be connected for life.

Your Shared History

There is usually a profound connection between two people that share experiences together throughout a good portion of their lives. Friendships come in all shapes and sizes. Today, you may have some good friends whom you may not see again until a few years from now. You may possibly never speak with them again as well.

Alternatively, you may make friends tomorrow whom you will know and care about well into your retirement years.

Most people find that the older they get, the more they cherish the friendships they have with friends they've had the longest. They may also deeply appreciate the friendships they still have with friends they might have been closer with when they were younger. No matter how many close friends you have and no matter how consistent those friendships may be, you may remain connected in some way in the future.

Making new friends can be wonderful. However, the feeling of sharing memories with an old friend hardly compares to having just met someone yesterday. For example, having just met a friend on a social network may be great, but it may not be as meaningful if you compare him or her to one of your childhood friends.

Life can be busy, and when even your closest friends' priorities and lives change, the friendship may lose its strength and momentum. Both friends may decide to focus on and invest more toward other relationships. They can still remain connected online with the option of revitalizing the relationship in the future. Friendships can come and go. They can also still mean something special to two old friends when they reunite after years of being totally disconnected.

The Importance of Loyalty

Loyalty is when you give or receive constant support and allegiance. Like personal chemistry, being loyal can't be faked

Going to college provides an opportunity to meet new people. One's college years are often considered among the best years of life.

or forced. It comes naturally and is based on the personal decision of how much one values another person. The more important a friendship is to you, the easier it is to be loyal. Being loyal is also easy to do when you know that loyalty is

Doing Things Together

The more experiences friends share, the richer their relationship can become. Friends who meet face-to-face and build their friendship in person will more likely have a deeper connection. They can still share and communicate online like they do with their online friends, but having the opportunity to share experiences together will bring them closer.

There are so many differences between having friends in life compared to having friends online. People have the freedom to enjoy both general types of friends. However, there's nothing quite like being in the same room with a friend and experiencing the same thrilling, scary, or even mundane things together. What makes only having online friends less satisfying than having friends in life is that there are limitations on what online friendships can offer. You can share content and communication online, but what about everything else you do in your life?

Sure you can capture your experiences on video and send them later or share a real-time or live video conference from practically anywhere. However, you're still not doing these things together in person. Doing things together in person is usually so much more satisfying. Even so, there will always be great value to having online friendships as well. There are online relationships where you also share telephone conversations. And still, you may also meet up in person once or twice a year.

Remarkable friendships lead to unforgettable memories as a result of the variety of experiences in life and online that friends share together.

important to the health of a friendship. You don't have to be a psychologist to know that motivation reflects the desires of a person. Those desires are based on the value system he or she has. So when it comes to sustaining a friendship, you can often recognize how much a friend values your relationship based on how he or she treats it.

For example, take two great friends who have known each other since kindergarten. While they may not have as much in common as they did while growing up, their shared history, similar interests, and similar senses of humor can still make being friends fun. But what happens when one of them goes off to college or moves across the country? It's possible that the friendship could suffer from such big life changes. Even the best friendship in life can evolve into a completely online friendship.

One of the easiest ways to prevent the loss of a friendship is to be a consistent friend. Doing this is simple when you make a consistent effort to maintain your relationship. You can do this even if you're thousands of miles apart and don't have constant access to the Internet. If you value the friendship enough, you'll still want to proactively be part of your friend's life. And what happens if your friend isn't interested? As previously mentioned, nothing is guaranteed when it comes to friendships. That's what makes having best and longtime friends so special.

Treating Your Friends Like Family

One of the benefits of having family members is the likelihood that they will be some of the few people with whom you'll have the longest history. Another benefit is the commitment that

Some of the most important and lasting friendships one can have are with family members. They're the ones who usually know you best and whom you can trust the most.

family members share with each other. While friendships can come and go, the relationships people have with their families are more likely to last because of their special bond. Imagine if you could combine the benefits of having a family with the benefits of having friends. While you may never live together, approaching your friendships from a position of being like family will probably make your relationships even stronger.

Many times, when conflicts arise within families, they are committed to working out their challenges. When problems come about within friendships, they may only be resolved if the relationship is worth it to both parties. Friends can eventually, easily, and often be replaced.

Treating your friends like they're family members is more likely to occur further down the line when the friendship is very strong and very important to you. The benefits of treating your friends like they're family includes knowing that you will most likely be willing to work things out with them during hard times. It also means that you're committed to having a long-term and possibly lifelong relationship with them as well. You know your friendship has the potential for being a lifelong relationship when you realize that you consider your best friends extended family members.

GLOSSARY

ACQUAINTANCE Someone known only slightly.

AUTHENTICITY The ability to be one's true self.

CHEMISTRY The natural and mutual attraction and compatibility between two people.

COMPASSION Sympathy or concern with regard to another person's unfortunate situation or circumstances.

COMPATIBILITY The ability for people to be friends harmoniously without conflict.

COMPONENTS The parts of a whole.

COOPERATION Working together in harmony.

DECIPHER To figure something out.

ENTREPRENEURIAL Related to business.

FUNDAMENTAL Of or relating to primary principle on which something is based.

INTENSIVE Vigorous in nature.

OPPORTUNITY A chance to do something.

PERSPECTIVE How something is viewed.

PROFOUND Very intense.

RESENTFUL The state of feeling or being bitter for having been treated unfairly.

REVITALIZING Giving something vitality.

SELF-DEPRECATING Being humorously critical of oneself in a playful and jovial way.

VERGE An edge or border.

VULNERABLE Open to attack or harm.

FOR MORE INFORMATION

Alumni Channel
419 Woodland Avenue
Cherry Hill, NJ 08002
(609) 471-3580
Web site: http://www.alumnichannel.com
Alumni Channel is an organization that offers alumni groups an easy
    way to get organized, keep active, and grow. The services it
    provides are great for people starting an alumni group or those
    who already have an organization set up and running.

Chai Friendship Club
6995 Westbury Avenue
Montreal, QC H3W 2X9
Canada
(514) 344-2424
The Chai Friendship Club is a department of the Chabad Lubavitch
    Youth Organization of Montreal that supports friendship
    between teenagers.

Dale Carnegie Training
780 3rd Avenue # C1
New York, NY 10017
(212) 750-4455
Web site: http://www.dalecarnegie.com
Dale Carnegie Training offers a variety of self-development courses,
    including "Effective Communications and Human Relations/
    Skills for Success." Dale Carnegie wrote *How to Win Friends
    and Influence People*.

Egyptian Canadian Friendship Association (ECFA)
879 St. Charles Avenue

Laval, QC H7V 3T5
Canada
(450) 687-0273
Web site: http://www.ecfriendshipassociation.com
The ECFA was established in 1990 to build a connection
between Egyptians who relocate to Canada. The organization fosters loyalty to both countries while embracing the
differences between their cultures.

Friendship Force International
127 Peachtree Street, Suite 501
Atlanta, GA 30303
(404) 522-9490
Web site: http://www.thefriendshipforce.org
Friendship Force was founded in 1977 and is active in over fifty
countries. The organization promotes friendship as well
as goodwill by supporting travel exchange programs.
Friendship Force has more than three hundred clubs
worldwide.

Girl Scouts Alumnae Association
Girl Scouts of the USA
420 Fifth Avenue
New York, NY 10018-2798
(212) 852-8000
Web site http://www.alumnae.girlscouts.org
The Girl Scouts Alumnae Association is provided by Girl Scouts
of the USA. It's an online community for alumnae to reconnect and stay connected, as well as to make new friends
that share the same affinity.

International Friendship Association
Leo R. Dowling International Center
Indiana University
111 S. Jordan Avenue
Bloomington, IN 47405
(812) 855-7133
Web site: http://www.indiana.edu/~ifa
The International Friendship Association is an organization at
Indiana University that fosters friendship among a diverse
group of people attending the school. It also promotes
different cultures, develops awareness, and educates
others on diversity.

Masada Maccabi Israel Summer Programs
15 East 26th Street
New York, NY 10010-1579
(212) 481-1500
Web site: http://www.hillel.org/hillelapps2/partners/partner.
aspx?agencyid=18219
The Masada Maccabi Israel Summer Programs is a nonprofit
organization that offers educational programs. It offers
Jewish youth the opportunity to explore the country of Israel
through a variety of experiences. The programs typically
include cultural, social, outdoor, and educational activities.

NAMI Queens/Nassau Friendship Network
1981 Marcus Avenue, Suite C-117
Lake Success, NY 11042
Web site: http://www.friendshipnetwork.org
The Friendship Network, whose focus is friendship, is sponsored
by the National Alliance on Mental Illness of Queens/

Nassau, New York. It is a social organization for single people twenty years or older who suffer from a mental illness and feel lonely and isolated because of their illness.

Scouting Alumni and Friends
Boy Scouts of America, National Council
P.O. Box 152079
Irving, TX 75015-2079
Web site: http://www.scoutingfriends.org
The Scouting Alumni and Friends organization is affiliated with the Boy Scouts of America. The organization helps BSA alumni and friends connect and reconnect with others that were once part of the organization.

Web Sites

Due to the changing nature of Internet links, Rosen Publishing has developed an online list of Web sites related to the subject of this book. This site is updated regularly. Please use this link to access the list:

http://www.rosenlinks.com/cwc/frnd

FOR FURTHER READING

Aitchison, Steven. *Making Friends: 8 Steps to Making Friends Quickly and Easily: How to Make Friends and Be Comfortable with Yourself*. North Charleston, SC: CreateSpace, 2010.

Boothman, Nicholas. *How to Make People Like You in 90 Seconds or Less*. New York, NY: Workman Publishing, 2008.

Capacchione, Lucia. *The Creative Journal for Teens: Making Friends with Yourself*. Pompton Plains, NJ: Career Press, 2008.

Carnegie, Dale. *How to Win Friends and Influence People*. New York, NY: Simon & Schuster, 2009.

Carnegie, Donna Dale. *How to Win Friends and Influence People for Teen Girls*. New York, NY: Fireside, 2005.

Covey, Sean. *The 6 Most Important Decisions You'll Ever Make: A Guide for Teens*. New York, NY: Fireside, 2006.

Csoti, Marianna. *Overcoming Loneliness and Making Friends*. London, England: Sheldon Press, 2006.

Desetta, Al, ed. *The Courage to Be Yourself: True Stories by Teens About Cliques, Conflicts, and Overcoming Peer Pressure*. Minneapolis, MN: Free Spirit Publishing, 2005.

Horchow, Roger, and Sally Horchow. *The Art of Friendship: 70 Simple Rules for Making Meaningful Connections*. New York, NY: St. Martin's Press, 2006.

Lowndes, Leil. *Goodbye to Shy: 85 Shybusters That Work*. New York, NY: McGraw-Hill, 2006.

Lowndes, Leil. *How to Instantly Connect with Anyone: 96 All-New Little Tricks for Big Success in Relationships*. New York, NY: McGraw-Hill, 2009.

Nelson, Linda. *Friends of Choice*. North Charleston, SC: CreateSpace, 2010.

Pace, Tom. *Mentor: The Kid & The CEO*. Edmond, OK: MentorHope Publishing, 2007.

Paul, Marla. *The Friendship Crisis: Finding, Making, and Keeping Friends When You're Not a Kid Anymore*. New York, NY: Rodale Books, 2005.

Shapiro, Lawerence E., and Julia Holmes. *Let's Be Friends: A Workbook to Help Kids Learn Social Skills and Make Great Friends*. Oakland, CA: New Harbinger Publications, 2008.

Taylor, Julie. *The Girls' Guide to Friends: Straight Talk for Teens on Making Close Pals, Creating Lasting Ties, and Being an All-Around Great Friend*. New York, NY: Crown, 2010.

Willard, Nancy E. *Cyber-Safe Kids, Cyber-Savvy Teens: Helping Young People Learn to Use the Internet Safely and Responsibly*. San Francisco, CA: Jossey-Bass, 2007.

Wolfe, L. Diane. *Lori* (The Circle of Friends, Book 1). Pikeville, NC: Dancing Lemur Press, 2009.

BIBLIOGRAPHY

Barton, Bree. "Are We Losing Empathy?: In Our Disconnected Society, Compassion Is Being Sacrificed on the Altar of Social Media." *USA Today*, October 20, 2010. Retrieved February 28, 2011 (http://www.usatoday.com/printedition/news/20101020/column20_st1.art.htm).

Blanton, Brad. *Radical Honesty, the New Revised Edition: How to Transform Your Life by Telling the Truth*. Stanley, VA: SparrowHawk Publications, 2005.

Borba, Michele. *Nobody Likes Me, Everybody Hates Me: The Top 25 Friendship Problems and How to Solve Them*. San Francisco, CA: Jossey-Bass, 2005.

Chapman, Gary. *The 5 Love Languages: The Secret to Love That Lasts*. Chicago, IL: Northfield Publishing, 2010.

Comm, Joel. *Twitter Power: How to Dominate Your Market One Tweet at a Time*. Hoboken, NJ: Wiley, 2009.

Cooper, Scott. *Speak Up and Get Along: Learn the Mighty Might, Thought Chop, and More Tools to Make Friends, Stop Teasing, and Feel Good About Yourself*. Minneapolis, MN: Free Spirit Publishing, 2005.

Creighton, Allan, M. Nell Myhand, and Hugh Vasquez. *Making Allies, Making Friends: A Curriculum for Making the Peace in Middle School*. Alameda, CA: Hunter House, 2003.

Ginsberg, Scott. *The Power of Approachability*. St. Louis, MO: HELLO, my name is Scott!, 2005.

Gorman, Melanie. "5 Signs It's Time to Kick Your Friendship to the Curb." Huffington Post, June 2, 2010. Retrieved February 28, 2011 (http://www.huffingtonpost.com/melanie-gorman/toxic-friendships-5-signs_b_597041.html).

Gottlieb, Hildy. *FriendRaising: Community Engagement Strategies for Boards Who Hate Fundraising but Love Making Friends*. Tucson, AZ: Renaissance Press, 2006.

BIBLIOGRAPHY

Hartley-Brewer, Elizabeth. *Making Friends: A Guide to Understanding and Nurturing Your Child's Friendships*. Cambridge, MA: Da Capo Lifelong Books, 2009.

Koval, Robin, and Linda Kaplan Thaler. *The Power of Nice: How to Conquer the Business World with Kindness*. New York, NY: Crown Business, 2006.

Lowndes, Leil. *How to Talk to Anyone: 92 Little Tricks for Big Success in Relationships*. New York, NY: McGraw-Hill, 2003.

Martinet, Jeanne. *The Art of Mingling*. New York, NY: St. Martin's Press, 1992.

McGibbon, Amalia, Lara Vogel, and Claire A. Williams. *The Choice Effect: Love and Commitment in an Age of Too Many Options*. Berkeley, CA: Seal Press, 2010.

McGinnis, Alan Loy. *The Friendship Factor: How to Get Closer to the People You Care For*. Minneapolis, MN: Augsburg Books, 2004.

Ostrow, Adam. "Social Networking Dominates Our Time Spent Online." Mashable.com, August 2, 2010. Retrieved February 28, 2011 (http://mashable.com/2010/08/02/stats-time-spent-online).

Price, Craig. *Half a Glass: The Realist's Guide*. New York, NY: Blooming Twig Books, 2010.

Qualman, Erik. *Socialnomics: How Social Media Transforms the Way We Live and Do Business*. Hoboken, NJ: Wiley, 2010.

Van Grove, Jennifer. "Facebook Now Tries to Tell the Story Between Two Friends." Mashable.com, October 28, 2010. Retrieved February 28, 2011 (http://mashable.com/2010/10/28/facebook-friendship-pages).

INDEX

About the Author

Jared Meyer is a speaker and author who helps people improve their decision-making and communication skills. As a marketing professional, he has been hired by communications companies and big brands to build relationships with thousands of consumers. He also teaches people how to build better relationships with their customers. Meyer has spoken at high schools and universities where he has provided keynotes and workshops on topics like Unforgettable Marketing, Opportunity Overload, and Dangerous Ambition. *Making Friends* is his seventh book. He may be contacted at info@jaredmeyer.com.

Photo Credits

Designer: Nicole Russo; Editor: Nicholas Croce
Photo Researcher: Marty Levick